Andy Albertini

ROGUE LEADERSHIP

By
ANDY ALBERTINI

Andy Albertini

Rogue Leadership
Andy Albertini

Published By Parables
June, 2019

All Rights Reserved. No part of this book may be reproduced or utilized in any form or by any means, electronic or mechanical, including photocopying, recording, or by any information storage and retrieval system, without permission in writing from the author.

    ISBN 978-1-945698-33-0
    Printed in the United States of America

Readers should be aware that Internet Web sites offered as citations and/or sources for further information may have been changed or disappeared between the time this was written and the time it is read.

Rogue Leadership

By
Andy Albertini

Andy Albertini

Rogue Leadership

TABLE OF CONTENTS

Table of Contents — Page 1

Introduction — Page 5

Section 1. Theology of Transformational Leadership — Page 7

Section 2 Section 2. The Change Management Process of Nehemiah — Page 17

- 2.1 - When who you are at your core begins to change, go with it! — Page 17

- 2.2 - If you can't dream it, you won't do it! — Page 25

- 2.3 - If it were easy, everybody would do it! — Page 33

- 2.4 - If you can make yourself understand what your true motivation is, accomplishing your goals will come easy! — Page 39

- 2.5 - Putting it all together and developing your strategy for metamorphosis. — Page 45

Section 3. The Fable — Page 51

Appendix — Page 68

STOP!

Before going any further, would you please read the fable that starts on page 51? I know this seems counterintuitive to most of us. Not to mention, I have a good friend named Shannon who horrifies me regularly by reading the last chapter of a novel first. So, I understand your pain. However, I promise it will all make sense in due time.

Dedication

This book is dedicated to the hardworking change agents languishing in the middle of some bloated org-chart waiting for your time. You are amazing, and I believe in you! You are the untapped resource that most organizations never notice but desperately need. Just know that I see you, and you can do it! **Your time has arrived, go Rogue my people!**

Thanks

This book would not be possible without the love and support of my wife Stephanie, and my two amazing kids Gabriel and Regan. You are my Why!

To my professors at Barclay College, thank you for believing in me, even when I didn't believe in myself.

Finally, I want to thank Bernie and Judy, my parents, for the example you were to me every day. In your own way, each of you typified what it means to be a great leader. I love and miss you both.

Introduction:

I was unaware of just how ragged and thin an edge I was running. My work was quite literally killing me. I was in the same unenviable position that many of the ministry executives, pastors, and business leaders I have spoken with find themselves. I was exhausted, burnt out and completely oblivious to my own condition! Like most of us, I had far too much to do, too little help and precious few resources to get things done.

I have interviewed dozens of senior ministry leaders and business people, and universally I hear the same concerns:

- We are facing the need to change the way we (Insert the thing that is keeping you up nights here).
- I can see that the culture has shifted around me. How do I restructure what we do?
- I know we need to change, but I have tried and been severely rebuked by my leadership.
- We made some changes, but in the end, we just went back to business as usual. It was just easier.

Interestingly I had uttered all these phrases and more, in the two years prior to starting this project.

I know what it is like to spend countless, sleepless hours staring at the ceiling looking for answers that would not come. Today, I am a bit of a specialist in the change world. I helped turn around troubled organizations. I would lead for several years then pass along a healthy organization to the next person. I have successfully accomplished this with Churches, 501c3's and one US Pharmaceutical Salesforce.

Leaders I speak with, without exception, tell me that they want to change and become better at what they do. However, very few make that leap. Most become upset that change creates too much pain and requires them to be personally transformed, a process that they neither understand nor appreciate.

As a result, I have felt the desire to create a Biblical model to aid all of us in the management of change. Helping organizations to become transformational organisms that will become more like Jesus for the sake of others is my passion!

One final note. You do not need to be a believer in any theology for this to work. All you must do is be a believer in truth. From my perspective, all truth is God's truth. However, from your perspective, you may simply find it easier to say that I have looked at ancient wisdom and found truth in what I studied. Faith is not a requirement for the process to be effective, but it will help a lot. If you have questions about your personal spiritual journey, I would love to talk to you about that as well. **I'll even buy the coffee!**

THEOLOGY OF TRANSFORMATIONAL LEADERSHIP

*"With man this is impossible, but with God
all things are possible."*
- Matthew 19:26

In Leading Congregational Change, by Herrington et al, we find this admonition, "The nature of leadership that is required to initiate and guide transformation represents a major shift for many. The leadership skills that most leaders have been taught or have "caught" are generally inadequate for this challenge." For this reason, I believe that a solid, biblically based, "Theology of Transformational Leadership" is now and will continue to be a vital tool for organizations to have and understand. If not, they have no hope of ever meeting the ever-changing demands of a society steeped in diversity and propensity for change.

Most of our organizations have become the place where change goes to die. Perhaps that is an overstatement, but when compared to the exponential rate of change within the broader society in which we live, it can certainly appear that change is nonexistent. Sir Winston Churchill once put the idea this way, "Change is good as long as it is in the right direction!" What catches most of us is the belief that almost all change is bad. As Shakespeare said, "Lord, we know what we are, but know not what we may be."

To combat this sense of disquiet that we feel during a time of change, our human mind has developed coping techniques. The human brain consumes about 25% of our daily energy when it is actively engaged. Think of the last time you had to learn something new and technical. Did you feel like your brain was hurting? The other key to our disquiet is that the human brain is designed to efficiently conserve calories and keep us alive. So then to avoid the expenditure of an additional 25% of our calories, we have perfected the art of "Change Aversion." Quoted in INC. Magazine, author Tim Ferriss says, "...people would rather be unhappy than uncertain." Neuroscience research teaches us that uncertainty registers in our brain much like an error does. It needs to be corrected before we can feel comfortable again, so we'd rather not have that hanging out there if we can avoid it.

The result of all this change aversion is that we have entered into "transactional leadership" agreements with most of our organizations. The transactional model of leadership is one in which leaders get compliance from a series of rewards and punishments that drive behavior. AKA the carrot and stick.

This way we all know who we are, and what we are expected to do, and as a result, we get outraged when those boundaries are tested. Under the status quo - everyone is happy, nobody gets hurt, and our brain gets to conserve calories. Win – Win – Win!

Having laid out the case for a need to develop a transformational leadership theology, I will look at Christ as the perfect model in Scripture to use as our example.

Transformation is a process that requires us to be in the moment. Therefore, a transformational leader is aware of Christ in him and around him. From 1 Chronicles 12 we hear of such transformational leaders, "From the tribe of Issachar, there were 200 leaders of the tribe with their relatives. All these men understood the signs of the times and knew the best course for

Israel to take." This is much more than a philosophical statement. Very rarely can transformation happen in a vacuum or accidentally. This presence cannot simply be described as an awareness of one's surroundings. Awareness of our surroundings are vital for transformation, but this awareness will come as a direct result of understanding that it is wholly predicated on the understanding that our very "being" is lived out in the presence of God. This is an important distinction. The former relies on our human ability to remain in the moment, while the latter allows God to put us into this state of "being."

Richard Foster, in "Life with God" says this, "We begin by opening our lives in the Christian community to the influx of God's life, and by experientially finding, day-to-day, how to let Jesus Christ live in every dimension of our being. The aim is not external conformity, whether to doctrine or the deed, but the reformation of the inner self."

Again, we must turn our attention to the one in whom all of history finds its meaning, the Lord. Jesus, who speaks of himself in the book of John, as "I AM!" This phrase in the original Greek is simply "ego eimi" which is a first-person singular tense of the verb "to be." We find in Strong's Concordance this explanation, ego eimi will "convey "straight-forward" being (existence, i.e., without explicit limits). We can draw great inspiration for our own leadership by allowing the self-described "ego eimi Jesus, to lead us to a place of being without explicit limits! This is Foster's reformation of the inner self! This is the beginning of a transformational leader, one who recognizes the majesty of God at the moment and allows that to wash over every aspect of their being.

As we progress in our understanding of remaining in the moment with Jesus, we will find the natural outcome of that closeness to be a love and respect for who He is and what He has done for us. Proverbs Chapter 1 provides an exceptional picture of this dynamic. We find that "The Message" provides a deep and rich perspective on this passage. "Start with God—the first step in learning is bowing down to God; only fools thumb their noses at such wisdom and learning." For the transformational leader, there is a great lesson to be learned from starting with God. All that we are and all that we can hope to become whether, in business, a ministry or even personally, finds power and meaning in Jesus!

It is this singular act of humbleness that provides the pressure relief valve for the pride that one can feel. This act of humble awe and reverence unto Christ ensures that we are exhibiting the high moral standard of Christ for our people to model. We are not just pointing the direction to go, but blazing the trail along with our followers, owning a sense of dependence on Christ and therefore that peculiar humility and personal drive that we aspire to.

Within a solid "Theology of Transformational Leadership," the result of such dependence on God will naturally guide the leader in developing an honest assessment of personal holiness and humility. Matthew 5: 48 commands a level of achievement that must come from God's actions, not our own. "But you are to be perfect, even as your Father in heaven is perfect." Again, in Leviticus 19:2, "Give the following instructions to the entire community of Israel. You must be holy because I, the Lord your God, am holy." Perfection is not a standard which any human being, except Jesus, can hope to achieve. Is this then a lost cause? Not at all. As I have stated before, as the Messiah, the Christ, only Jesus could live this command out perfectly. In this teaching, He sets up for us, not a new unattainable standard, not a re-visitation of the law that is impotent to deal with our sin. But rather a new way of looking at righteousness that is empowered by the Spirit, through the Son at the command of the Father. The transformational leader must tap into this dynamic of personal holiness not based on the innate ability of the leader himself/herself. Rather we need to lean into the ability of Jesus to transform!

This leaning into the righteousness of Jesus finds expression in Ephesians 5:1, "Imitate God, therefore, in everything you do, because you are his dear children." From a theological standpoint, we can infer from these scriptures that this personal holiness is not so much a destination, as it is a process. Part of the leader's "being" from above is dedicated to walking daily, humbly, empowered by the spirit. Our spiritual formation, becoming like Jesus for the sake of others, is foundational to this theology.

In addition, if we are as transformational leaders seeking to be imitators of God, we must again look to Jesus as our example. How did Jesus live out his personal holiness? We must ask the question, "Did Jesus live a life of piety that was proactive or exclusionary?" The answer gives us great insight into the proper place of holiness in a Theology of Transformational Leadership. N.T. Wright said this about the expectations people had of our "Lord Jesus'" message. It consisted in the announcement that the time of fulfillment had now dawned. The kingdom of God, long-awaited, was now at hand. He saw himself and was seen by his contemporaries as a prophet, bringing God's word to his people. But a good part of his ministry was devoted to explaining, in word, symbol, and deed, that although the nation's aspirations were now, at last being met, the fulfillment was not as expected."

It is like Wright suggests, Jesus was in all ways unexpected. Please note, Wright points out for us, that Jesus showed us how the kingdom was to be fulfilled in word, symbol, and deed. I believe this points to a very proactive view of holiness. To be transformed and at the same time being transforming, the leader must seek to express holiness in action versus inaction, in doing versus abstention. We must express our holiness as an extension of Jesus' work on earth, to comfort the afflicted and afflict the comfortable.

The Apostle Paul points out in Philippians 3:12, "I don't mean to say that I have already achieved these things or that I have already reached perfection. But I press on to possess that perfection for which Christ Jesus first possessed me." A transformational leader presses on to possess that very thing which Jesus has called them to. I refer to this as your "Why", but more on that later.

With such an understanding of personal holiness, the leader can rest in the knowledge that there is a great deal of security in Jesus. It is my belief that only with that kind of dependence on Jesus and security in His ability to complete a work that he has begun in us, that we can become genuinely vulnerable with those that follow us. "We now have this light shining in our hearts, but we ourselves are like fragile clay jars containing this great treasure." 2 Corinthians 4:7 This makes it clear that our great power is from God, not from ourselves.

By allowing ourselves this clay pot vulnerability, we can escape the trap that ensnares so many leaders such as isolation and arrogance. It has been said by someone that, "the only two places you can hide your heart from pain are heaven and hell." Leadership of any kind, but especially transformational leadership, opens the leader up to critique. When we try to hide, we lose the ability to connect with and learn from our followers. By modeling this kind of vulnerability, we allow our followers to develop the same trust in us, which we have in Jesus. This will establish a very freeing environment in our organizations. I have often said none of us is as smart as all of us. As we employ these leadership techniques, we should allow our people both the access to approach us as well as the freedom to fail. In one word, that means vulnerability.

Service to others is the natural outcome of a Transformational leader that is vulnerable because our security is in Jesus and as a result, we do not need to fear those around us. This, in turn, allows for a spirit of service to develop in the group. In Matthew 20:28, we see once again the Master lovingly guide us in the right path, "For even the Son of Man came not to be served but to serve others and to give his life as a ransom for many." Transformational Leaders are not interested in a top-down, autocratic style of administration. Jesus leads us into a model that says we, as an organization, must serve the far greater purpose God has set forth for us. Transformational leaders live in submission to Jesus as King and strive to call others into mutual submission. The temptation for the leader is to focus on the portion of the organization that seems to go along with no encouragement necessary. However, Matthew reminds us that it is dangerous to simply serve the easy to serve. Transformation, once started in the leader, will push us to become servants of the difficult and unpleasant as well, for the sake of right relationships in the kingdom and for the glory of God.

To say that such vulnerability and service to the unlovely is difficult would be far too great an understatement. Transformational leaders cannot accomplish this task in their own strength. Just as with personal holiness, there is a complete dependence on the redeeming work of Jesus, so here we need to acknowledge that in all things the transformational leader must have a deep dependence on Jesus Himself. John 15:5 says, "Yes, I am the vine; you are the branches. Those who remain in me, and I in them, will produce much fruit. For apart from me you can do nothing." Jesus sets the standard for the leader to strive for here. Stay connected to me, and I will do all that is necessary through you. The branch alone is of no value except perhaps as a decoration. Far too many leaders end up as a dry, dead, and well-preserved figurehead.

Life, health, vitality, strength, and support are all provided to the branches by the vine alone. The fruit of any organization can be predicted by the connectedness of the leader to Jesus. This fruit is the outcome of our connectedness to Jesus. Our fruit alone, grown in our own effort will be despoiled by time. Shakespeare said of the human body, "I have wasted time and now time doth waste me!" Such is the nature of temporal things, but the things of God will far outlast any leader. This should be our goal, that the work of the organization far outlasts us. This end is only possible if the leader and the organization stay connected to Jesus. Transformational leaders also encourage their individual followers to stay connected to the vine. When this is accomplished, Jesus is glorified by the leader, the followers and the organization.

How then does the transformational leader accomplish all of this? A transformational leader is empowered by the Spirit. Consider the life of Jesus again. Frequently the Gospel writers tell us that Jesus would draw away from the crowds and listen to the Father speak through the Spirit. For his whole life, Jesus was connected to the Father through the spirit. Jesus was conceived by the power of the Spirit (Luke 1:34–35), was empowered by the Spirit for ministry (Acts 10:38), led by and fought temptation by the Spirit (Luke 4:1–2), taught in the power of the Spirit (Luke 4:14), and Jesus was empowered by the Spirit to heal (Luke 5:17). If Jesus is indeed to be our model for transformational leadership can we be any less empowered?

The spirit is the promise of our inheritance. He will lead, guide and direct us as leaders. Jesus promised as much in Acts 1:8a, "But you will receive power when the Holy Spirit comes upon you." That power is from God, and it is for God's glory. As transformational leaders we must be empowered so that we can, in turn, have transformational organizations, resulting in God being glorified!

The goal of this theology of transformational leadership is to inspire us to see Jesus in a way that causes real and lasting transformational spiritual formation. The reason being is so that we will pick up this definition of spiritual formation, becoming more like Christ for the sake of others!

Here are three steps you can use to become a transformed leader:

1. Get unvarnished feedback. Look for a mentor, a great teacher or loved one who can give you an honest, perhaps even brutally honest, assessment of your strengths and weaknesses. If all else fails, spend a couple of bucks and get a good personality inventory. I prefer the "Leading from your Strengths Profile."

2. Know thyself. Start by taking some time to understand your life as a story. Ask yourself, "Who am I and why am I like this?" This exercise will give you insight into your current self, as well as let you see how you approach your future.

3. Walk through the process. At Rogue Leadership we take people through the process of Core Change – Dream – Apply Effort – Transform others.

If you have made it this far, you are already considering your core change. Next, think through what worthy dream you can create for your leadership journey. Then apply effort to make that dream a reality!

Reflection Questions

"This is what He showed me: The Lord was standing by a wall that had been built true to plumb, with a plumb line in his hand. And the LORD asked me, "What do you see, Amos?" "A plumb line," I replied. Then the Lord said, "Look, I am setting a plumb line among my people Israel..." Amos 7: 7-8

My grandfather was a stone mason. A plumb line was a way to guide the mason to build a wall that would be strong and last a lifetime. Masons will often use the phrase, "lay to the line" as a way of teaching a novice how to stay true to the build.

What is your plumb line?

How much time per month do I spend in self-reflection?

If I were to create a dashboard for my personal growth what would it look like?

Do I see myself the way Jesus sees me?

Do I see my team as Jesus sees them? What does that look like?

Do I see my team as Jesus sees them? What does that look like?

The Change Management Process of Nehemiah

2.1 When who you are at your core begins to change, go with it!

"Life is a series of natural and spontaneous changes. Don't resist them; that only creates sorrow." - Loa Tzu

We must begin at the beginning. For change management, that is the moment you realize that who you are at your core has begun to change. This represents a new birth, or at the very least a realization that some profound change has begun. Core shifting is a painful and sometimes dangerous process. "Child survival rates have increased dramatically since 1990, during which time the absolute number of under-five deaths has been slashed in half from 12.7 million to 6.3 million, according to a report released today by UNICEF." From a global perspective, the singular act of being born is one of the most dangerous things a human being can do. In change management, this moment, the moment of realization, is equally dangerous. Why? Because if this opportunity is mishandled the entire process begins sick and anemic. Andy Crouch likens the process of changing culture to the first breaths of a newborn child. "You emerged wrinkled and wet, squinting against the light. You wailed in a thin and raspy voice, taking gulps of unfamiliar air until someone placed you near a heartbeat you knew even better than your own." In 2011 Steve Denning, a contributor to Forbes Magazine, writing for his personal blog post said, "In a bureaucracy, problems can fester for years, or even decades before anything is done about them. Such unresponsiveness is incompatible with the goal of delighting clients. Radical transparency both within the team and management is a necessary basis for continuous innovation. Management by enablement and dynamic linking provide some of the practices needed to establish radical transparency, including daily standup meetings, the systematic identification, removal of impediments, delegation to the team of how much work to undertake, and providing a clear line of sight for everyone in the organization to the client."

It is in this crucial moment that a truly transformed leader must emerge and start the culture shift. This process can be likened to a ship that is seeking to navigate across a vast ocean. The transformed leader sees that a course correction is necessary. However, in a journey of 10,000 miles, one does not simply approach the helm, grab the wheel and give it a spin, as we see in the movies, rather subtle changes are made so that over the course of the journey the correct destination is found. Likewise, cultural change in such a rapid fashion is frequently dangerous and foolish as well. Mr. Denning pointed out that problems can lie festering for long periods of time. Transformational leaders may be willing to see and feel the need for change in such a way that we can communicate the need, to create a healthy sense of urgency but not induce panic in the system. Nehemiah was such a transformational leader. In Nehemiah 1 we see this interaction:

"In late autumn, in the month of Kislev, in the twentieth year of King Artaxerxes' reign, I was at the fortress of Susa. 2 Hanani, one of my brothers, came to visit me with some other men who had just arrived from Judah. I asked them about the Jews who had returned there from captivity and about how things were going in

Jerusalem. 3 They said to me, "Things are not going well for those who returned to the province of Judah. They are in great trouble and disgrace. The wall of Jerusalem has been torn down, and the gates have been destroyed by fire."4 When I heard this, I sat down and wept. In fact, for days I mourned, fasted, and prayed to the God of heaven."

First Nehemiah was changed as we discussed in the section on Theology of Transformational Leadership. In his prayer, we see humility and a broken heart. This man was nothing more than a disposable canary in a coal mine, yet we see in this prayer the shaking of a man's core to the point that something snapped. Nehemiah no longer accepted his fate as a disposable servant. He has been reborn as a transformational leader. For leadership to effectively change the culture of their respective organizations, there must be a corresponding transformation within the leaders. Look at what Nehemiah did. He sat down in shock and horror, meditated on the problem, and asked God to make a change.

I know that we all want to believe that we can be part of something bigger than ourselves. Look inside and access that part of yourself, the part that still dreams. The part we are told as we grow is "silly" or "idealistic" and the parts that the "Experts and Elites" of the world hate. They tell us you must sell out your dreams to be considered a responsible adult.

Remember change is a variable, not a constant!

Conventional wisdom for the past 2500 years as popularized by Heraclitus says, "Change is the only constant." Far be it from me to disparage ancient wisdom. In fact, I regularly study it to gain fresh insights into modern problems. However, in this case, I must admit that the modern world has changed sufficiently to warrant a new look at this old cliché.

Change, contrary to popular belief, is not a constant. It is very much a variable. The velocity of change is growing at an exponential rate. Just when you think you have it nailed down to a predictable formula, it takes a giant leap forward.

Accordingly, if the rate of change inside your organization is not at least roughly approximating the velocity of change in the world around you, you're in trouble. These quantum leaps in innovation, AKA "disruptive innovation" are going to affect every organization out there sooner or later. Look at this report from Bain Capital in their February 2018 Insights Newsletter that predicts 1 in 4 jobs will be gone by the end of the 2020's. So, what then is to be done? Far too many organizations we see place their heads firmly in the sand and declare everything is going to be fine.

To demonstrate this problem, allow me to use the following example. From the beginning of recorded history, humanity has striven to work our way up Maslow's Hierarchy of Needs. These five interdependent levels of basic human need must be satisfied in sequence starting with the lowest level. Physiological needs for survival (to stay alive and reproduce) and security (to feel safe) are the most fundamental and most pressing needs. These 2 needs, in particular, have been satisfied in large part to the discovery and use of fire.

From "Og" the caveman to the height of the Bronze Age in 1500 B.C., nothing really changed in the human use of fire. It was the primary way to heat the home and cook your food. From the Bronze age to the Viking era in the mid – 700's A.D., very little changed in the human use of fire. It was still the primary way to heat the home and cook your food. The same process remained at the beginning of the American Revolution in 1776. Fire still heated our homes and cooked our food. However, within 37 years (1783-1820) the advent of the modern stove had arrived.

This took almost 3500 years of recorded history. Change in that day and age came in long slow waves. You would have had decades if not centuries to prepare for what was coming next. This is not so today. In the modern era, we are faced with a much more rapid velocity of change. A freshman in college studying computer science will have to come to grips with the fact that what they learned in that first year of adulthood will be obsolete by the time they graduate in 5 years. Some studies we have looked at recently suggest that obsolescence is occurring every 14-18 months.

In reality, we are either equipping leaders for challenges that will be irrelevant in a few short months or years, or we are going to have leaders that will be equipped to lead in an organizational structure that does not yet exist, dealing with problems we can't even begin to imagine, with tools that won't be created for another 5 years.

So, here are 4 velocity accelerators you can implement today:

1. Kill your EGO! One of the biggest problems we see leaders wrestling with is that of EGO. If your organization is going to increase its internal change velocity, you will need to get out of the way. All too often leaders are the bottleneck in an organization. Change your focus to understand the "Why" of change. Trust your team to see the problem better than you can and then the solution will emerge. Be the guide and not the hero.

2. Embrace a flattened hierarchy. In the same vein as the death of your ego, let the need for a steep org-chart die. Get out of the sage on the stage mentality and dream with your team. The people on your frontline have way more information than you do

in the manager's office. Remember none of us is as smart as all of us.

3. Let go of your old decision-making model. Most leaders only know and understand the "Transactional Model" of leadership. I despise this model unless you need to give short-term urgent information. The transaction model looks like this: Leaders see the need to make a change, so a decision is discussed amongst the highest levels of leadership. A roll out to the staff happens. Affected staff members are asked for feedback. Carrot and stick strategies enforce that change. Everybody loses, because this kind of change effort will fail 67% of the time according to Harvard Business School. (Don't blame me for this one!)

Instead, consider implementing a transformational model of decision making. Who you are at your core starts to shift, and you notice the need for change. Leadership meets to discuss a change effort matrix (fig 2). Staff closest to the frontlines are asked for input and creative ideas (dream with your team), then you make a decision. Change is initiated and benchmarked on key initiatives. Have your team celebrate milestones and adjust as necessary.

Refection Questions

1. What about my sense of self-perception is holding me back from seeing the core shift happening around me? Do I think of myself as too important or not important enough?

2. What are the environmental factors (AI, Technology, Culture, etc.) that are causing the core shift?

3. How am I going to initiate transformation within myself so that I can lead the change in my organization?

4. How does God see me? What does that change about how I see myself?
(see Fig 1 Positional Truth)

Andy Albertini

2.2 If you can't dream it then you won't do it!

"Through Hard work, perseverance and faith in God, you can live your dreams." – Dr. Ben Carson

In the movie "A Knights Tale" the main character born a commoner in feudal England asked his father if it was possible for a man to change his stars? Several spectators in the crowd laughed at the boy and told him that it was impossible. The father simply replied, "Yes." For those of us who are leading change efforts for our organizations, we will find those around us who would scoff at our desire for change. In this, as in all areas of life, we need to accept humbly the feedback of those around us but take everything with a proper grain of salt. Learn from the experts. Solicit their opinion, but keep in mind that many who achieve the level of power and prestige that great notoriety can bring, all too often end up smug or slothful in their own growth. All of this leads to the next step in managing change.

If you can't dream it, you won't do it. Dreams are very powerful things. Dreams and dreamers are truly the great drivers of cultural change in any organization. C.S. Lewis once said, "You are never too old to dream another dream." Frequently we find that organizational culture gets stuck. I have likened this concept to that of a caterpillar that dreams of flight. In truth, not all caterpillars that can transform into a butterfly do. I suppose that the analogy breaks down just a bit here because of the environmental factors that affect the insect world, but this much I know to be true, some organizations don't transform into their potential selves because they lack the ability to dream.

"The mass of men lead lives of quiet desperation." -- H.D. Thoreau. I read this quote a long time ago, and it was not until I began my studies of metamorphosis that it began to ring true! It has become my experience that most organizations exist at about 70% of the possible effectiveness that could be experienced. Organizations become complacent without powerful dreams, like individuals they exist without passion. Individuals work at jobs they hate but continue to work because they cannot see any other options. They're just happy to have a job. They live in cities where crime and corruption run rampant because they have always lived there and ever so slowly, they have grown accustomed to the distress around them. Life and the powers that be, have inoculated them from the truth of what they could be, like getting a little of the flu virus in a flu vaccine, they have been given a little success. They are then told that it is the best they can expect, which in turn has caused them to become immune to genuine, bona fide transformation. They exist in a sick dreamless culture and have lost sight of the possibilities beyond. Andy Crouch in a discussion of living in the "Wilderness" vs. living in a "Theme Park" makes a sage point. After the creation story in Genesis, God "removes" himself and allows Satan a chance of tempting the man and woman with the power of knowledge. While I find knowledge a perfectly useful thing, it has been my experience that it pales in comparison to dreaming. Dreams that transform us are powerful tools in change management and culture making. Dreams tell us what can be. Dreams are mostly responsible for all innovation in the world around us. Crouch likens this to a gardener who plants and tends a well-ordered garden that will produce good fruit. I believe that dreams can have the same effect on our culture.

    I have heard that the director of the U.S. Patent office in the late 1800's said that the office should be closed because in his opinion, "Everything that can be invented already has been invented!" I have also heard that this is not a true statement. Either way, it represents a sad but true mantra in far too many organizations and individuals. Those who say, "We can't" or that, "We shouldn't!" This negativity tends to hang over us like smog over L.A. For my money any and all predictions of future events should be looked at as nothing but a pack of lies. Nobody knows the future except God alone. So, if we are going to lie about it, why not make it a positive lie? Do not be mistaken. I am not suggesting that we put on rose-colored glasses, but let's also acknowledge that things are not nearly so grim as we make them out to be. As change creators, we need to keep realistic but positive dreams in front of our people and at the same time keep the dreams of the people in front of the leaders.

As Nehemiah was changed, he began to dream a dream that would transform the very culture around him. "Early the following spring, in the month of Nisan, during the twentieth year of King Artaxerxes' reign, I was serving the king his wine. I had never appeared sad in his presence. 2 So the king asked me, "Why are you looking so sad? You don't look sick to me. You must be deeply troubled. "Then I was terrified, 3 but I replied, "Long live the king! How can I not be sad? For the city where my ancestors are buried is in ruins, and the gates have been destroyed by fire."4 The king asked, "Well, how can I help you?" With a prayer to the God of heaven, 5 I replied, "If it pleases the king, and if you are pleased with me, your servant, send me to Judah to rebuild the city where my ancestors are buried."

How is it possible that a disposable person would approach the most powerful person in the world and make such a bold request? In a word… DREAMS!

I am a firm believer that you don't have to be someone like a Bill Gates to create seismic waves of change in the universe. You must simply know how to dream. The first step is to understand that you cannot do this in isolation. It is a rare thing to see a dream known only to one person become a reality. I am always quick to point out, "None of us are smarter than all of us!" John Quincy

Adams once said, "If your actions inspire others to dream more, learn more, do more and become more, you are a leader." Adams was correct about this because our dreams are far more powerful when they inspire those around us to action and that requires a community of people working together.

As leaders, we must grasp the power of this principle. Far too often senior leaders gather behind closed doors and talk/ strategize with each other then, send out status updates to the minions in the form of standup meetings or memos. There is some use in this type of structure. If you need to communicate real-time, important or urgent issues, then go for it.

On the other hand, I have been held hostage in enough weekly meetings where I was told, "Senior leadership is meeting and cooperating well together. Senior leadership is working as hard as they ever have and we feel like we are making good progress." We appreciate you and will be sending you an email about (insert pointless agenda item here)."

I kid you not! I have had that exact phraseology delivered to me at multiple jobs in multiple states. Managers seem to instinctively know how to talk nonstop and simultaneously say absolutely nothing.

Be warned, to talented people stuck in the middle of your organizational structure, these conversations sound a lot like, "sit still until the grown folk tell you what to do next." If you are doing this, please don't insult the intelligence of the people on your team by telling them that you want them to communicate back up the chain to senior leadership. Hint, hint- we can see right through this canard.

This is not dreaming together. This is transactional leadership at its finest, and that isn't very fine. You can probably tell I am not a fan of transactional leadership- it will suck the very soul of your team bone dry.

Here are three practical tips to start really dreaming with your people:

1. Develop your trust quotient. Your people will not dream with your organization until they believe that you want to listen to them and help them achieve their dreams in return.

2. Bring your employees a worthy goal. As leaders, we have a responsibility to show our team their hard work makes a difference beyond quarterly numbers. We all want leaders who can dream of something beyond themselves and look to create a broader reaching impact that extends into the community and influences society. Think about Apple as they set out to build the first iPhone.

3. Have Dreaming Sessions– You spent so much time recruiting a team that is humble, hungry, and smart. If you aren't letting them speak into the organizational direction, then their capacity and time become an opportunity loss and a sunk cost on the balance sheet. It is dangerous if only a handful of people have

all the best ideas. This is the reason your personal transformation as a leader is so significant.

Reflection Questions

1. Why did I want to do this _____ (ministry, business etc.) in the beginning?

2. When was the last time I asked my team to dream along with me?

3. A dream shared, becomes a plan. Who am I sharing my dreams with?

4. Does my team own the dream? If not, why? How do you know they own the dream?

5. Is the dream big enough to inspire my team? How about my audience, client, customer or board?

2.3 If it were easy then everybody would do it!

"By perseverance the snail reached the ark."
– Charles Spurgeon

Nehemiah understood that this request was a dangerous one, but he had a plan. "7 I also said to the king, "If it please the king, let me have letters addressed to the governors of the province west of the Euphrates River, instructing them to let me travel safely through their territories on my way to Judah. 8 And please give me a letter addressed to Asaph, the manager of the king's forest, instructing him to give me timber. I will need it to make beams for the gates of the Temple fortress, for the city walls, and for a house for myself." And the king granted these requests because the gracious hand of God was on me."

Nehemiah reminds us that if changing culture was easy, everybody would do it. I recently read the text of a commencement address supposedly given by Bill Gates the founder of Microsoft. It was full of the kind of salient advice I wish I had listened to years ago. It was advice like, "Life isn't fair, get used to it!" Also, "The world won't care about your self-esteem. The world will expect you to accomplish something before you feel good about yourself." The path of a change agent is like this as well. It is fraught with peril. If you decide to make change a priority, don't expect the world to stand up and applaud. The world is full of people who cannot stand to see others succeed. We all have competitors who are trying to attack our product and steal our market share. Many of us have a boss or coworker who may grow jealous of our success and in the extreme case may even attempt to sabotage our progress.

In 1990 I was living in Daytona Beach Florida. My first Saturday on the beach revealed a curious behavior that I spent the summer watching with great interest. Black Finned Dolphins would show up just offshore, and the tourists from Ohio would see that fin in the water and move as fast as possible onto the beach, usually with a toddler or two under their arms.

At the same moment, locals were sprinting into the surf to get close to those same fins. The locals knew the difference between a dolphin fin and a shark fin, families from Ohio didn't.

While leading change efforts, you can expect similar behaviors from your employees at predictable intervals. Like their beach-going counterparts in Florida, you will observe groups in your organization moving at high rates of speed towards, or away from your change efforts. Those running headlong at the change are most likely those in your organization that are early adopters of change, or people with whom you have a great relationship. The clear majority, some estimates are as much as 80% will initially become like the scared tourists, running pell-mell away from your change efforts. This principle is known as the "Diffusion of Innovation."

This moment represents one of the very real danger points within your change efforts. The point at which your organization will try to defend the status quo by taking out the change agent at the knees. Great news, right? In many instances, the promise of change can seem an unfair bargain. Leaders ask their organizations to give up familiar and deeply held positions for a promise of better things in the future. This is a cause of perceived pain and, just in case you didn't know it, people in pain do stupid and dangerous things.

In the now infamous "Google Manifesto on Gender" one Google engineer created a rift of epic proportion. I am not here to re-litigate the veracity of the Jerry McGuire style rant, but I can observe that the manifesto was born out of an ever-increasing sense of loss and detachment from the changes that were manifesting in the Google culture. He was running for his life, away from what he perceived as a shark! The truth is, people will fight tooth and nail to avoid feeling pain.

So, what can you, as a leader, do to protect yourself and your organization during the high-stress moments in the change process?

Here are four steps that work:

1. As early as possible in the change process involve the stakeholders in the change. We talk about the fact that when who you are at your core begins to shift, go with it. This is the time to get your team together and explain what is happening. Then start dreaming with your team. There are, I promise, disruptive innovators in the ranks of your team, and you will be treated to ideas, solutions, and paths forward that you could never dream up alone on your best day. The change you are dreaming of will need new blood to come to life.

2. Over-communicate with your team. Leaders have a nasty habit of moving into silos with crucial information. Limiting access to the reality of what is going on leads to distrust and creates an environment that becomes a breeding ground for perceived pain and discontent. Rumors will begin to pop up like dandelions in the spring. The only antidote I am aware of is honest talk. By the way, *please* don't do "Town Hall Meetings!" These are trite and notoriously shallow. Putting management up on stage and

the groundlings below sets up a truly harsh dynamic and stifles what could otherwise be an excellent opportunity to have an honest conversation. Think King Arthur's round table, not the wise sage on the stage as your model.

3. Set up realistic and achievable goals for the team that make the most sense, and are aimed toward a feeling of progress and success that will act as fuel to keep the team pulling together for the sake of that grand dream you worked so hard to make real. At the same time start using the language of success. This is vital and will require you to be vulnerable and available to exhibit your own transformation as a leader. Start talking as if the goal has already been achieved and is a new reality! Find any excuse to throw a victory celebration and make that a regular part of the change process.

4. Give the proper incentives for the right behavior. The old adage applies here, what gets rewarded, gets repeated. A sad cliché to be sure, but it is a sad cliché for a reason. During any change effort, you are usually asking your team to sacrifice extra time away from their families or the loss of something else of importance to them. That alone is reason enough for you to take seriously the threat that you might just have to face a rebellion if this change pain is mismanaged. You will see some obvious symptoms that the team is gunning for you.

- The overall fashion quotient goes up. (People will dress better because they are taking interviews and you are at risk of losing talent.)

- Sick days and vacation requests start to rise for the same reason.

- A general slowdown of projects. Unfinished projects pile up, and the pressure on you rises as well.

- The rumor mill goes into overdrive!

Reflection Questions

1. If I have identified that a core shift is happening, have I involved my team?

2. Where am I on the decision process matrix? (Fig 3)

3. How is my team dealing with the change pain? How can I help them?

4. Is my own personal fear holding my team back? What am I afraid of?

5. What is my change threshold? (Fig 4)

Andy Albertini

2.4 If you can make yourself understand what your true motivation is then accomplishing your goals will come easy!

*"Ability is what you are capable of doing.
Motivation determines what you do."*
– Lou Holtz

We must understand that fear is a great killer of change. We become paralyzed into not making a move. Nehemiah was sad in the presence of the King. This fact alone could have cost him his life. The king's cup barer was there simply to keep the King from being poisoned. In West Virginia, where I grew up, the phrase, "Like a canary in a coal mine" referenced the custom of miners to keep canaries with them to detect odorless poison gas leaks. If the canary died, time to get out of the mine. Nehemiah was very much a canary in a coalmine to the king.

If the King was displeased with his disposable servant, Nehemiah, he could simply have Nehemiah killed and replaced with a "happy canary."

The question we must ask and answer here and now is why Nehemiah made the change. I assume others were equally distressed that the walls and gates of Jerusalem were in ruin. It is my firm belief that Nehemiah had found his true motivation. "17 But now I said to them, "You know very well what trouble we are in. Jerusalem lies in ruins, and its gates have been destroyed by fire. Let us rebuild the wall of Jerusalem and end this disgrace!" 18

Then I told them about how the gracious hand of God had been on me, and about my conversation with the king. They replied at once, "Yes, let's rebuild the wall!" So, they began the good work."

When Nehemiah began to voice his dream in light of his motivation, he immediately had the goodwill of his followers. First Nehemiah is transformed, and now his vision begins to transform those around him! Today we must refuse to use the term impossible! It is a statement. It is final! And if you believe it, then it is also true.

Long ago, or so it seems to my memory, I was working in the contract Pharmaceutical Industry. Unlike the stability created working for a large pharma company, contract pharma was an industry filled with uncertainty. In some ways, we were nothing more than a very talented, highly educated "rent-a-salesforce." A salesforce that could be eliminated as soon as the parent company needed to slash a little red ink from the books for an upcoming shareholders meeting.

What I observed was instructive. At regular intervals, and perhaps with the best of intentions, management would announce, "All is well. The contract is going to be renewed!" Which would immediately initiate a firestorm of rumor and panic in most of the salesforce. The result of this panic, people spent their time on the wrong things. (Mostly resume polishing and interviewing.) 9 times out of 10 things worked out fine, but these fear-filled individuals cost themselves dearly in terms of bonus money and advancement opportunity.

By allowing fear to drive them, they made fewer quality sales calls and saw a drop off their income as a result. Eventually, I would show up after their manager gave them a poor performance review and called me. My job as, National Organizational Effectiveness Manager, was to assess where they were at and either create a performance improvement plan or "coach them out" of the organization.

The brain's fear center is the amygdala, an almond-shaped part of the deep brain. "The amygdala isn't responsible for all of our fear response, but it's like the burglar alarm that connects to everything else, said New York University psychology and neural science professor Elizabeth Phelps."

Courageous questions are the antidote to fear. Look at our friend Nehemiah. The next question we must ask and answer is why did Nehemiah change? Something in his core had shifted. Remember, he was made aware that God's city, the thing that he loved most, was in ruin and God's reputation was in disgrace (his real motivation). As a result, he went into a time of prayer and self-questioning. I imagine the big questions he asked were, "If not me, who? If not now, when?" He knew that the place that his questions led could very well end his life. In this instance, you need not believe scripture to be true to see the application points of this story. The truth is the truth. We might also take some solace at this point in remembering that very few of us truly make life and death decisions.

Part of what I do, is help leaders become transformational. Transformation often involves how we use language. I never allow myself to contemplate the possibility of the impossible anymore. Instead, I ask, "Why will this change everything?" The difference is that of a question vs. a statement. A statement gives your mind permission to be lazy and shut off. Conversely, questions challenge its creativity. Questions open the world of possibility in a way statements never could. The trick is to allow your true motivation to ask the right kinds of questions!

You need to understand the power of the question, "Why?" Why unlocks the courageous conversations we all need to have.

Conversations that allow us to challenge conventional wisdom, break molds, take risks and change everything.

When you understand the why proposition, the solutions thinking will emerge. The problem is we tend to focus too much on the "how" side of the equation. How do we grow? How do we reach new people? None of these are bad questions in and of themselves, but they all miss the mark.

Think of this as a mathematical equation: $W? + TM = H$

(Why questions, plus true motivation = How.)

The question, "Why," must be answered first.

In her book Fierce Conversations, Susan Scott notes that "…my realization [is] that while no single conversation is guaranteed to change the trajectory of a business, a career, a marriage, or a life, any single conversation can." Such is the power of the concept of "why." This is a critical point. Scott sees it this way, "a fierce conversation is one in which we come out from behind ourselves into the conversation and make it real." That reality is vital to change.

So then how do we avoid such fear-driven mistakes? Questions…honest, courageous and bold!

Here are 4 needs that must be satisfied to encourage courageous questions in your organization:

> 1. The Need for Safety– A safe environment is paramount. You are asking your best and brightest to put a lot on the line. Jobs, family security, future promotions, etc. Ask yourself if your people feel safe enough to tell you that "one big thing" that can change everything for your organization.
>
> 2. The Need for Transparency– This cannot be about management's agenda. No political style push polls will get you the kind of information you need to answer the why portion of

the change equation. This cannot be agenda driven. Invite honest critique (see #1 above), and you will be amazed by how your people will amaze you. If you are open and transparent with your people, they will respond in kind.

3. The Need for Willingness– to go where the questions lead. No really! You have to be willing to walk this trail no matter where it ends. Trust me, if you are tapping into the collective mojo of your team, this will pay huge dividends.

4. The Need for a Guide– that can come in and help you manage the change pain that will result.

Reflection Questions

1. What do I need to do to increase my trust quotient with my team? Have I ever betrayed their trust in the past? Do I need to make amends to have courageous conversations?

2. In our current circumstance, what does transparency look like?

3. Can I identify specific information silos I have put in place that need to be broken down?

4. How will I respond if the conversation goes in an unexpected direction? Do I trust my team enough to follow through? If not, why not?

5. List 1 or 2 people you would like to have as a guide in this process. Make a specific plan to contact them.

2.5 Putting it all together and developing your strategy for metamorphosis.

"Planning is bringing the future into the present so that you can do something about it now."
– Alan Lakein

The final stage we see exemplified for us by Nehemiah is this, "Putting it all together and developing your strategy for metamorphosis." In Nehemiah Chapter 2 we see Nehemiah putting together his plan for metamorphic change! "11 So I arrived in Jerusalem. Three days later, I slipped out during the night, taking only a few others with me. I had not told anyone about the plans God had put in my heart for Jerusalem. After dark, I went out through the Valley Gate to inspect the broken walls and burned gates, but my donkey couldn't get through the rubble. So, though it was still dark, I went up the Kidron Valley instead, inspecting the wall before I turned back and entered again at the Valley Gate."

We must become intentional if the change is to be implemented. During my undergraduate studies at Malone University, Dr. Herb Dymale, one of my favorite professors, was fond of saying, "A mist in the pulpit will result in a fog in the pew!" In other words, we must be intentional and clear in our communication. Even the slightest "mist" in our clarity, will result in an impenetrable "fog" of confusion for our team.

Nehemiah took his time, got the lay of the land, made a plan and when he delivered that plan to the elders it was met with resounding support, despite the inherent danger such an undertaking would represent.

In the end, it took Nehemiah only 52 days to rebuild a wall that some estimates put at roughly 2.5 miles long, averaging 12-15 feet tall and 8-12 feet thick. This required a complete change in the culture of the people of Israel. From being ruined and defeated as a people to people willing and able to work with a trowel in one hand and a sword in the other.

I would note that the vast majority of the Nehemiahan System of Change Management that I have outlined takes place in the first two chapters of a thirteen-chapter book. To this end, I will point out again that the journey we go on as agents of change is very like a ship. We need to take our time and make sure that the course correction, small but intentional, puts us in the correct port when we arrive many, many miles later.

Final Encouragement!

"Yesterday I dared to struggle. Today I dare to win!"
- Bernadette Devlin

I love to build fires! I love cutting the wood, laying the kindling, striking the Ferro rod, blowing the newly formed ember into a flame and the smell of wood smoke on my coat the next day. It connects me back into something that has long left most of mankind, the wild.

Unlike my grandfather's generation, one of the safest places we can find ourselves these days is at work. Unless you are fishing crab off the Alaskan coast or work for the bomb squad. By the way, if you have either of those two jobs, you are officially Steve McQueen cool and I want to be your friend! Call me, we can hang out. If not, I will venture to say that most of us work in a safe environment, but hey! We can still hang out.

For the sake of this discussion, I'll call this environment the factory. Why? Because one way or another we all produce something just like in a factory. Factories, for the record, are dream killers! There is no real life to be found in the factory. Being in the wild invites us to dream and dare. You can't really dream in the factory.

I tell my children, either you live your dreams, or you will end up working for someone who is. If you can't dream something, you won't do it.

I want you to know that I understand what I am asking you to do. It is dangerous, daring and slightly frightening. I am certain that right now you are full up with "What-if Syndrome." What if I fail? What if this hurts my organization? What if this costs me personally?

The good and bad news here is that it will. I promise, you will fail, but remember that failing isn't fatal, not trying is. I promise you will hurt people in your organization, because change by its very nature is painful, but often just a simple admission that you let someone down and as a leader you will be accountable to perform better in the future will suffice to fix the problem. Do this publicly and I promise your team will respect your candor. Finally, I promise that this will cost you something personally, but you will grow and become a better version of yourself.

Leaving the relative safety of the factory for the wild is an inherently dangerous prospect. That is the reason most of us never take that step across the threshold of possibility. Unless we are willing to step out and live the best possible example of our God given dream, we are slowly dying on the factory floor living to make another man's dreams come true.

Are you ready to plan your exit from the factory floor?

- Brainstorm– Get a group of people you trust together for dinner at your house. During dessert ask them, what can you do better than anyone else?
- Research– The wild does not necessarily require a degree or specialized training. Just ask Bill Gates and Steve Jobs. What are you passionate about? You can become a subject matter expert at your local library for a couple of bucks in late fees.

- Build a tribe of followers. I would suggest you read Seth Godin's book, "Tribes."
- Set Smart Goals– Dream an amazing dream, then do something about it!

Andy Albertini

A Change Fable.

What Color Are Your Boots?

By Andy Albertini

Andy Albertini

What Color Are your Boots?

'Without continual growth and progress, such words as improvement, achievement, and success have no meaning."
-- Ben Franklin

It was unexpected. But then again it was always unexpected. Just like every other day for the last few years that darn alarm clock went off just in time to shake Walter out of his only respite from that little niggling feeling in the very back of his head that something was not quite right. He was still not able to put his finger on the problem, but there it sat none the less, just out of reach of Walter's consciousness like a faint shadow on an overcast day. It was definitely there, just a bit hard to identify. It gnawed at the edges of thought but never committed itself to come fully into the light of reason. "Well," said Walter to no one in particular, "No sense in lying here any longer. Might as well get up and get ready to go to work. I can't be late again, or the foreman will flip!" Walter got up and pulled on his six pair of shiny, black boots and headed out the door for work.

What's that you ask? How could Walter wear six pair of shiny, black boots at one time? Very simple. Walter was a caterpillar. He was born and raised on the side of the grand red brick house just beside the river, and he worked just like his father and grandfather before him in the big bush at the end of the street. Every day he would leave his warm comfy house and get in line with all the other caterpillars, in their shiny black boots, as they marched lockstep to the bush to gather nectar and eat leaves. Walter was a strange kind of caterpillar. Unlike the rest of his crew, he often stopped munching and crunching leaves just to stare off into space and think. He was also known for watching the bees as they went from flower to flower.

    Walter loved the idea of flying free, like the bees. Almost every time he watched he thought I wish I could do that. Once he had even made the mistake of telling his co-workers about a dream that he often had. He dreamed that he, plain old Walter, had taken flight and joined the bees for just one day. Looking down he saw for the first time the world he lived in and realized that there must be more to it than he had been led to believe. He was weightless, flying high above the ground. For the first time in his life, he felt free, really free! He was the master of his own destiny. Nothing could touch him up there; no cares for the day or problems at work. He was happy in his dreams. His crew on the bush had all made fun of Walter's dream of flight in the beginning. The truth was, now a year later they still did a good bit of ribbing at lunch if the opportunity arose. I guess that is how Walter got his nickname… Buzz!

    After a while, Buzz, as he was now known, learned to accept the name and the good-natured ribbing from the guys that was attached to it. So, things continued for a while just as they always had, or so it seemed to Buzz. Buzz would wake up at the beckoning call of his alarm clock, put on his shiny black boots and fall in line. It was coming up on the rainy season, Buzz's least favorite time of year. He always got in trouble this time of year, mostly for stepping out of line. Buzz could never understand why when the foreman stepped in a puddle everybody else had to as well. It made his boots all spotted with mud and water droplets that he would have to polish off later that evening. But that was the rule and to top it all off Buzz really hated working in wet boots. Well, who could blame him really? After all, one set of squishy feet can be extremely uncomfortable, but can you imagine 6? It was on a particularly gloomy day that Buzz, without even realizing what was happening, got a message from the edge of his consciousness. Glancing down at the leaf he had been munching on, a question had appeared, "What color are your boots?" Buzz looked around wondering who could have sent him such a strange message. For it was a bizarre message indeed, because for as long as anyone could remember caterpillars had always worn plain, black boots. Whoever had sent Buzz that message obviously did not know much about caterpillars, so Buzz decided to ignore the message! "After all," Buzz said, sounding very much like his father and grandfather, "It never paid to listen to silliness!" A lesson he had learned from the whole dream incident. But much to his surprise, the messenger would not be ignored.

    The very next day Buzz got another message, "I asked you a question... What color are your boots?" Feeling somewhat silly, but feeling that it might be rude to ignore the messenger any longer, Buzz whispered to no one in particular, "My boots are black."

    "Excuse me," asked Joe who was perched on the next leaf. "Of course, your boots are black, what color should they be?" "Sorry Joe, just thinking out loud" responded Buzz somewhat embarrassed.

    The next day Buzz actually woke up before his alarm clock sounded. Dressing quickly, he headed out into the rain and in no time at all he was back at the bush. He really did not know why, but he was expecting something to happen today. Expectation has a way of motivating that provides the necessary fuel for success.

After lunch, he looked down at the leaf he had been working on, and there was a third message. "WHY?" Well said Buzz, "I guess because I have always worn plain black boots." But the question forced Buzz to enter into a very courageous conversation with the messenger that stood resolutely on the edge of his consciousness. Buzz later realized that without the courage to ask the tough and uncomfortable questions, change, real change was impossible. Courageous conversations driven by courageous questions revealed real issues that would otherwise never see the light of day.

The next day as Buzz was working a particularly uninteresting piece of leaf, he noticed the bees in the distance, and he had one of these courageous conversations with himself "Why can't I do that?" Stopping short Buzz realized something. He never had, even in his dreams, considered the possibility of actually joining the bees and once more the messenger within spoke, "why not?"

"WHY NOT!" Buzz said. "How about because I DON'T HAVE WINGS!" But the thought would not go away. In fact, it seemed to have taken up residence in Buzz's spare bedroom like an unwelcome house guest, figuratively speaking of course. Soon, Buzz realized that he needed to do something to launch a change in his life or this messenger from the edge might never give him a moment's peace again.

Buzz spent the weekend doing something that no caterpillar, as far as he knew, had ever done. He knew instinctively that this would cause quite a bit of gossip. Perhaps even a hullabaloo, but he had also come to realize that he had to see it through! Courageous questions when answered honestly and with an eye toward transformation will always cause a tectonic core shift. So, Buzz added the most scandalous yellow and red flames to his plain black boots that he could imagine. He also made a sign for himself and hung it on the wall beside the door where he would see it every day. The sign said simply, "When who you are at your core begins to change, go with it!"

He had been asking himself the question for several days now, "I want to believe that I can be part of something bigger than myself. The real question is can I?" "Yes, I can," came his answer in the middle of a very sleepless night. "Indeed, I must!" But the question remained hanging in the air, "What is that something bigger going to be?" When he got in line the following Monday, the procession came to a crashing halt! "FLAMES," boomed a very surly voice! "That is unacceptable!" It was Buzz's foreman Al. He had worked with Buzz's father years ago on the line. After regaining his composure, Al said to Buzz in a much more clandestine tone. "Buzz, you know I go way back with your family. Heck, it was your Grandfather who got me onto this bush, but I can't keep covering for you. If you would just stay in line and not make so many waves, you could be supervising your own crew by now! Heck, you might even be in line for my job someday." Then looking back at the line, somewhat sheepishly, he bellowed. "Buzz you know we all wear plain black boots. This is most irresponsible and possibly even dangerous of you."

Buzz's only reply was to shrug his shoulder and ask, "WHY?" But the question went unheard as the line had begun moving again and the thump, thump, thump of the many booted feet drowned out all but his own thoughts.

Later at lunch, he explained his new-found philosophy to his co-workers, although he was sure most of them would never understand. "The flames on my boots, Buzz expounded, are there to remind me that fire radically changes things, even on an elemental level. So, if I keep a fire lit in myself, there is still time to drastically revolutionize who I am. It is possible. You see, it is never too late to reinvent who you are. I refuse to believe that you have to sell out your dreams to be considered dependable. I refuse to be afraid of change anymore. Sometimes the most responsible thing you can do is make a hard choice like this and be somewhat reckless." Buzz finished passionately!

    Buzz knew that his life would never be the same from this point on and he was excited to see what the visitor on the edge of his consciousness was going to teach him next.

"A mediocre idea that generates enthusiasm will go further than a great idea that inspires no one." - Mary Kay Ash

Buzz's dreams of flight had begun to occur with much more frequency and stunning realism than they ever had before. It was as though some long-dead part of him had all of a sudden been resurrected while at the same time his fear of the unknown future had vanished. Buzz had begun to live an authentic life. No more hiding behind the mask of civility and being what the world told him he should be. Buzz realized that a profound part of himself was being transformed. Buzz looked around at his friends and co-workers, and almost none of them were really and truly happy.

Buzz predicted that most were only seventy percent as happy as they would be doing something else. They complained, just like Buzz used to, about not liking their jobs or their boss or their life in general, but were for some reason, unwilling to trade the security of the familiar for real zeal in life! They spent way too much time and energy blaming their circumstances on external things. In short, they all had dreams they were unwilling to pursue. Sure, they all had very noble sounding reasons for not doing anything. "I'm close to retirement or someday, but right now I have to stay here and do this or even what if I try and fail?"

Buzz made up his mind that nothing was going to stand in his way. Dreams, it seemed to him, were the fuel for creativity and creativity was the key to living above the seventy percent line in life. That afternoon Buzz got a message from the edge of his consciousness. It said simply, "Dreams are the beginning of your reality." Buzz liked that, and when he got home, he made another sign by his door that said "If you can't dream it, you won't do it!"

After all, Buzz reasoned, the future is still yet to be written. Any predictions about the future will only be accurate if I let them be!

Over the course of the next several months, Buzz started to formulate his plan. Something had to change. The routine Buzz had fallen into needed to be drastically altered. Buzz learned about a term called "Mumpsimus!" A mumpsimus it seems is a traditional custom or notion adhered to although shown to be unreasonable. Buzz reasoned that we all have at least a couple of mumpsimus' in our lives that keep us stuck in a place where change is impossible. Sure, he reasoned, the changes would be painful, draconian even, but changing was seldom easy.

On his days off and in the evenings, Buzz spent countless hours studying the bees. What made them do what they did? Where did their motivation come from? Their thinking it seemed to him was not simply different from his, but it went so far as to seem alien. He had no idea that fellow insects could be so different. They did not work in beautiful straight lines, but they still seemed to work as a team. They were all independent, yet they all worked for the common good of the hive. At first to Buzz, it all looked like chaos, but as he studied, he saw patterns and predictability. He realized it was more like a well-orchestrated dance than a group of insects working in the linear fashion he was accustomed. One communicating to the other where the flowers were located, drones carrying pollen back to the hive, yet there was no need for an apparent central command structure. Everybody knew their job, and everybody did it. They functioned as a team, inspired by a singular worthy goal. This inspiration then became the basis for the group to establish a plumb-line for future efforts and successes.

It occurred to Buzz that this was going to be a lot harder than he initially thought. It was no longer a matter of just learning to fly. It meant that his whole outlook and philosophy on life was going to need to change.

How was he going to be able to break the bounds of Earth if he couldn't understand why and how the bees flew? He was sure that if he could just replicate the process of the bees the mystery of flight would be magically unlocked.

Buzz's co-workers had begun to notice that he was acting strangely, even for him. They would see him with a pad and pencil heading out early every weekend to watch bees. He was always taking notes, muttering to himself about the power of a transformation. Some began to worry that he had lost his mind. Others began to avoid him altogether. It didn't take Buzz long to figure out that he was being "forgotten about" when the crew went out after work. He stopped getting polite invitations to polite parties. All the while he was growing increasingly frustrated with the progress he was making on his flight plan. He had in his notebook, designs, drawings, calculations, and theories but he was no closer to seeing his way clear to flight than he was at the beginning.

"Success is no accident. It is hard work, perseverance, and sacrifice.
"- Pele

Buzz was getting a little down one Sunday afternoon when the long silent voice from the edge of his consciousness reappeared just as suddenly as it had exited. "If it were easy, everybody would do it," said the voice. This thought comforted Buzz. "You're Right," he said out loud and added the phrase to the others that now took up quite a bit of space on the wall by his front door. The rainy season had slipped into what should have been a beautiful warm summer for Buzz. However, Buzz would only remember the frustration and seeming lack of progress on his flight plan that took prominence in that that season.

Buzz had filled notebook after notebook with designs, drawings, notes, plans, and sketches. On one particularly exasperatingly difficult evening, he decided he needed to take a walk to clear his mind. As he walked by the river, his thoughts ran to the apparent problem. For all of his plans and schemes, hopes and aspirations, sketches and designs, he was absolutely no closer to taking flight! "How in the world will I ever get airborne?" Buzz thought in desperation.

He had secretly conducted a few tests. He had built a set of bee wings out of wood and canvas as a first prototype. As it turned out the wings were too small and too heavy. That had proven to be a painful lesson. The next generation of his design was lighter and bigger, but he realized that they lacked any real aerodynamic properties of lift and thrust. Version 3.0 included some pyrotechnics! Suffice it to say that version 3.0 left an indelible mark on Buzz.

Buzz realized too late, that bee wings were not the answer. Seemingly, up to and including all years from 1909 until 2019 even scientists couldn't explain how bee wings worked. So, Buzz reasoned after a lengthy stretch in the library, and bird wings would be the answer for version 4.0. Unfortunately, version 4.0 proved just as disastrous as all the others. "How, how, how was the mantra that had become Buzz's all-consuming thought. He was absolutely sure that change was necessary for his life. He knew that core change was the only way he could see the dream of flying come to fruition. He even understood that hard work and genuine, honest effort on his part was necessary for his own transformation.

In a moment of crisis, he had even given up for a few months. Insisting that he had been foolish for thinking that he could ever fly. "Maybe they are right after all" he reasoned. "What have I gotten for all of this nonsense? No social life, no promotions at work and lots and lots of frustration."

Buzz had decided that the cost of transformation was too high. It was more natural and less painful to chalk the whole thing up to a lesson learned and just dive head long back into the rut he had lived in for so long. It was at this time that the mysterious visitor from the edge of Buzz's thought made a most unexpected return.

> *"So I say to you, Ask and it will be given to you; search, and you will find; knock, and the door will be opened for you."*
> - Jesus Christ

"You are asking the wrong question!" the voice practically screamed. "Where have you been," demanded Buzz. "I have been trudging and slogging through all of this because of you, and you were as silent as the tomb!"

"I have been here, watching and always with you, never very far away," said the voice in a way that made Buzz believe him. "I thought you had left me for good," Buzz replied.

The voice told Buzz that, "Sometimes the hard work of trudging and slogging was necessary. It was the time in the change process that most turn back. Fear, apathy, and pain have a way of halting progress." The voice continued, "It is at this point that far too many stop dreaming and start asking how, which is the wrong question."

The voice explained that by declaring victory and stopping the dreaming process, or by allowing ourselves to lapse back into the old patterns and ruts we would naturally start to ask, how do we change? The correct question is not how but "WHY?"

Why unlocks the courageous conversations we all need to have. Buzz determined that courageous conversations allow us to challenge conventional wisdom, break molds, take risks and see those dreams as a reality.

When you understand the why questions in life the "how thinking or solutions thinking," will emerge noted the voice. The problem Buzz decided was that he, like most of us, tend to focus too much on the "how" side of the equation. Our human nature makes us especially bad at this. We want to fix problems and stop pain. We ask how questions to get to the solution without really understanding the problem. How do we grow? How do we get new customers? How do we reach new people? None of these are bad questions in and of themselves, but all of them miss the mark of the real question. "Why" must be answered first.

In all honesty, thought Buzz, understanding your why thinking, or true motivation is paramount. Buzz had decided that the best motivation he had for his true motivation, was to make life better for someone else. If he could change himself into a being that could fly, who knows how that might make things better for others? "Become a transformed person," thought Buzz, "so that you can become a transformer in the world."

Buzz also started asking new questions, "Who needs my help? Whose life can I touch?" By tapping into those motives, Buzz found that the pain of trudging and slogging was significantly reduced if not eliminated.

Later that night Buzz added a new sign on his wall. "If you can make yourself understand what your true motivation is then accomplishing your goals will come easy!"

"We are all butterflies. Earth is our chrysalis."
- LeeAnn Taylor

It wasn't very long after that Buzz was having one of those courageous conversations at lunch with the guys. Joe seemed particularly interested in the apparent changes that had taken place in Buzz.

Gone was the old Walter that seemed like he was living a pie in the sky dream of flight. He was different, but Joe just wasn't sure exactly how. Joe was lost in his own thoughts. Buzz spoke up. "So, like I was saying, I have the feeling that this is about much more than me getting airborne. I think it is about all of us in some way. I can't really explain it yet, but I know that this is about all of us."

In truth, most of the guys felt uncomfortable with this new and improved Buzz. One problem Buzz noted to himself was that when you live out of your authentic self, people can get uncomfortable.

As the summer passed into fall, Buzz had not heard from the voice, but he knew he was close and watching over him. He also became vaguely aware that there was a growing sense of expectancy emerging in him. He knew something BIG was about to happen, but he was not sure when or how, but he was certain it would be soon!

On the first real clear, crisp fall day, Al was impatiently waiting for Buzz to get in line so that his crew could start the long march to the bush. However, on this day Buzz wasn't just late, he was absent! Al made a fair attempt to rouse Buzz by pounding on his front door, but nobody answered. The scene repeated itself for the rest of the week. As much as Al hated to do it, he had to write

Buzz up and have him fired. The letter notifying Buzz of his severance was returned unopened.

Not only was Buzz absent from work, it appeared as though he had disappeared altogether. It was as if he had just vanished. Joe had ventured over to Buzz's house just once and peaked in the front window. Everything looked o.k., but he thought he caught a glimpse of something weird hanging from the bedroom ceiling.

That had been over a month ago. Joe finally decided somebody needed to go check out Buzz's house. What if Buzz had been the victim of an accident or foul play? In a very uncaterpillarly way, Joe threw caution to the wind and broke into Buzz's house through the front door with a crash. The scene that presented itself defied any explanation.

Buzz was nowhere to be seen, but in his bedroom was a creepy translucent shell. There didn't seem to be any evidence of foul play, which relieved Joe, who honestly liked Buzz. After searching the rest of the house, Joe decided Buzz was probably gone for good. He thought of all the good times that had together and feeling somewhat uncharacteristically sentimental decided to grab a pair of Buzz's flaming boots for a keepsake. As he turned to walk out the door, he noticed all the signs Buzz had made. So, he decided to take them as well. He hung the signs on the wall in his den in the same order he found them.

When who you are at your core begins to change, go with it!

If you can't dream it, you won't do it!

If it were easy, everybody would do it!

If you can make yourself understand what your real motivation is, accomplishing your goals will come easy!

If you can expand your mind to see infinite possibilities, you will be transformed.

Joe spent a lot of time that winter looking at those handmade signs and flaming boots. The memories that they brought back to him were warm and funny. He truly missed his friend. When spring arrived once again, Joe was back on the bush when he noticed the bees, but he also noticed that among the bees was a striking butterfly. It seemed odd to him, but he had work to do and decided that he had best get back to it. As he turned to head a little deeper into the bush, a voice from the edge of his consciousness asked, "What color are your boots?"

"To accomplish great things, we must not only act but also dream; not only plan but also believe."
- Anatole France

Time to put this whole thing together. I was inspired to write this little book because, after two decades of ministry and business experience, I have seen that our teams are suffering. Leaders need a real and Biblically based system to adapt and change to the world around them. The truth is most organizations lack the skills to adapt. We stick with what we know, even if it stops working. That is called a mumpsimus.

Does that sound familiar to you? In far too many meetings I have been a part of, it comes out like this: "We must not become worldly, or we have always done business this way!" There are hundreds of variations on this theme, and I am sure you can name many from your own experience. So, the courageous question I want you to ask is this, "What would your organization look like if God were to transform it through you?" In other words... "What color are your Boots?"

Appendix:

"Bible Suite." November 1, 2013. Accessed November 1, 2013. http://biblesuite.com/greek/1510.htm.

Crouch, Andy. Culture Making: Recovering Our Creative Calling. Madison: IVP Books, 2013.

Denning, Steve. "Steve Denning." N.p., n.d. Web. 3 Nov. 2014. <http://stevedenning.typepad.com/steve_denning/2011/01/reinventing-management-part-5-from-value-to-values.html>.

Harvard Business Review (2011-02-24). HBR's 10 Must Reads on Change Management (including featured article 'Leading Change,' by John P. Kotter) (Kindle Location 2995). Perseus Books Group. Kindle Edition.

Herrington, Jim, Mike Bonem, and James H. Furr. Leading Congregational Change: a Practical Guide for the Transformational Journey. San Francisco: Jossey-Bass, 2000.

Holy Bible: New Living Translation. Gifted. Tyndale House Publishers, Inc., 2006.

Holy Bible: New Living Translation. Carol Stream, IL: Tyndale Publishers, 2006. Print.

Krejicer, Roger. "Church Leadership. Accessed February 25, 2015. http://www.churchleadership.org/apps/articles/default.asp?articleid=42346&columnid=4545

"N.T. Wright Page." November 8, 2013. Accessed November 8, 2013. http://ntwrightpage.com/Wright_NDCT_Jesus.htm.

Peterson, Eugene H. The Message: the Bible in Contemporary Language. Numbered ed. Colorado Springs, CO: Message, 2005.

Shakespeare, William, and Paul Werstine Ph.D. Richard Ii (Folger Shakespeare Library). Edited by Dr. Barbara A. Mowat. Simon & Schuster, 2005.

Shakespeare, William. Hamlet (Folger Library Shakespeare). New York: Simon & Schuster, 1992.

"UNICEF." Accessed October 31, 2014. http://www.unicef.org/media/media_75893.html.

Zondervan. Life with God: Reading the Bible for Spiritual Transformation. New York: HarperOne, 2010.

Fig 1.

2 Corinthians 5:17

Therefore, if anyone is in Christ, he is a new creation. The old has passed away; behold, the new has come.

Galatians 2:20

I have been crucified with Christ. It is no longer I who live, but Christ who lives in me. And the life I now live in the flesh I live by faith in the Son of God, who loved me and gave himself for me.

1 Peter 2:9

But you are a chosen race, a royal priesthood, a holy nation, a people for his own possession, that you may proclaim the excellencies of him who called you out of darkness into his marvelous light.

John 1:12

But to all who did receive him, who believed in his name, he gave the right to become children of God,

Romans 12:2

Do not be conformed to this world, but be transformed by the renewal of your mind, that by testing you may discern what is the will of God, what is good and acceptable and perfect.

John 15:5

    I am the vine; you are the branches. Whoever abides in me and I in him, he it is that bears much fruit, for apart from me you can do nothing.

Colossians 3:3

    For you have died, and your life is hidden with Christ in God.

Galatians 3:26

    For in Christ Jesus you are all sons of God, through faith.

1 Corinthians 12:27

    Now you are the body of Christ and individually members of it.

John 15:15

    No longer do I call you servants, for the servant does not know what his master is doing; but I have called you friends, for all that I have heard from my Father I have made known to you.

1 Corinthians 6:19-20

    Or do you not know that your body is a temple of the Holy Spirit within you, whom you have from God? You are not your own, for you were bought with a price. So, glorify God in your body.

Romans 8:17

And if children, then heirs—heirs of God and fellow heirs with Christ, provided we suffer with him in order that we may also be glorified with him.

2 Timothy 1:7

For God gave us a spirit not of fear but of power and love and self-control.

Romans 8:37

No, in all these things we are more than conquerors through him who loved us.

2 Corinthians 2:14

But thanks be to God, who in Christ always leads us in triumphal procession, and through us spreads the fragrance of the knowledge of him everywhere.

Romans 8:1

There is therefore now no condemnation for those who are in Christ Jesus.

Philippians 1:6

And I am sure of this, that he who began a good work in you will bring it to completion at the day of Jesus Christ.

Romans 8:16

The Spirit himself bears witness with our spirit that we are children of God,

Colossians 3:12

Put on then, as God's chosen ones, holy and beloved, compassionate hearts, kindness, humility, meekness, and patience,

Galatians 3:26-28

For in Christ Jesus you are all sons of God, through faith. For as many of you as were baptized into Christ have put on Christ. There is neither Jew nor Greek, there is neither slave nor free, there is no male and female, for you are all one in Christ Jesus.

Romans 8:28

And we know that for those who love God all things work together for good, for those who are called according to his purpose.

Galatians 3:27

For as many of you as were baptized into Christ have put on Christ.

1 Corinthians 3:16

Do you not know that you are God's temple and that God's Spirit dwells in you?

Andy Albertini

Ephesians 2:10

For we are his workmanship, created in Christ Jesus for good works, which God prepared beforehand, that we should walk in them.

There are 2 attributes of change we need to think over, "Onset Speed and Predictability."

Predictability, speaks to how far in advance you know that the change is coming.

Onset Speed speaks about the velocity of onset resulting from that change.

The relative effort of your team climbs as the predictability and onset speed change.
Fig 2

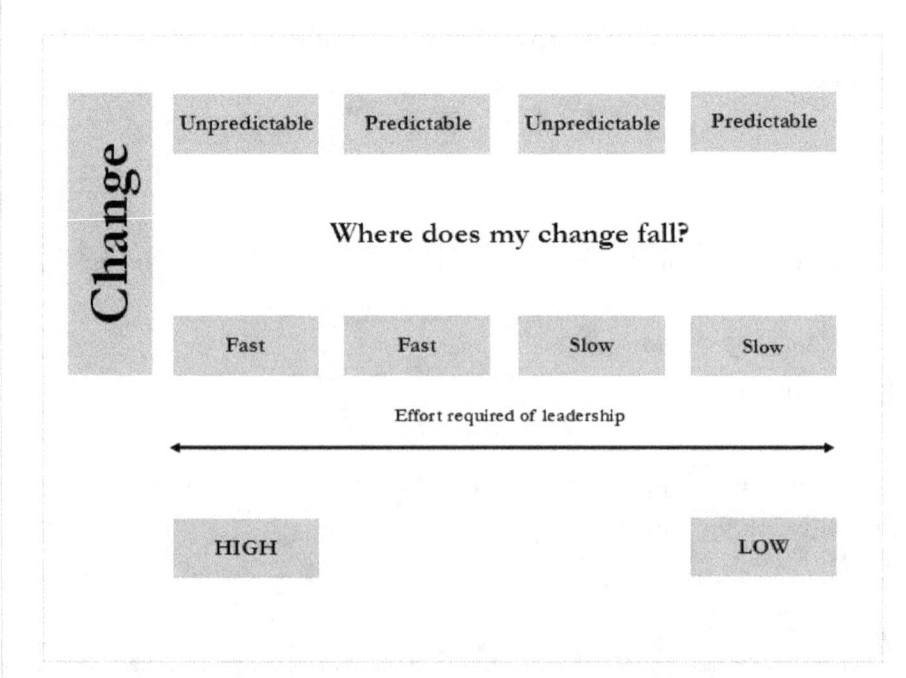

Fig 3

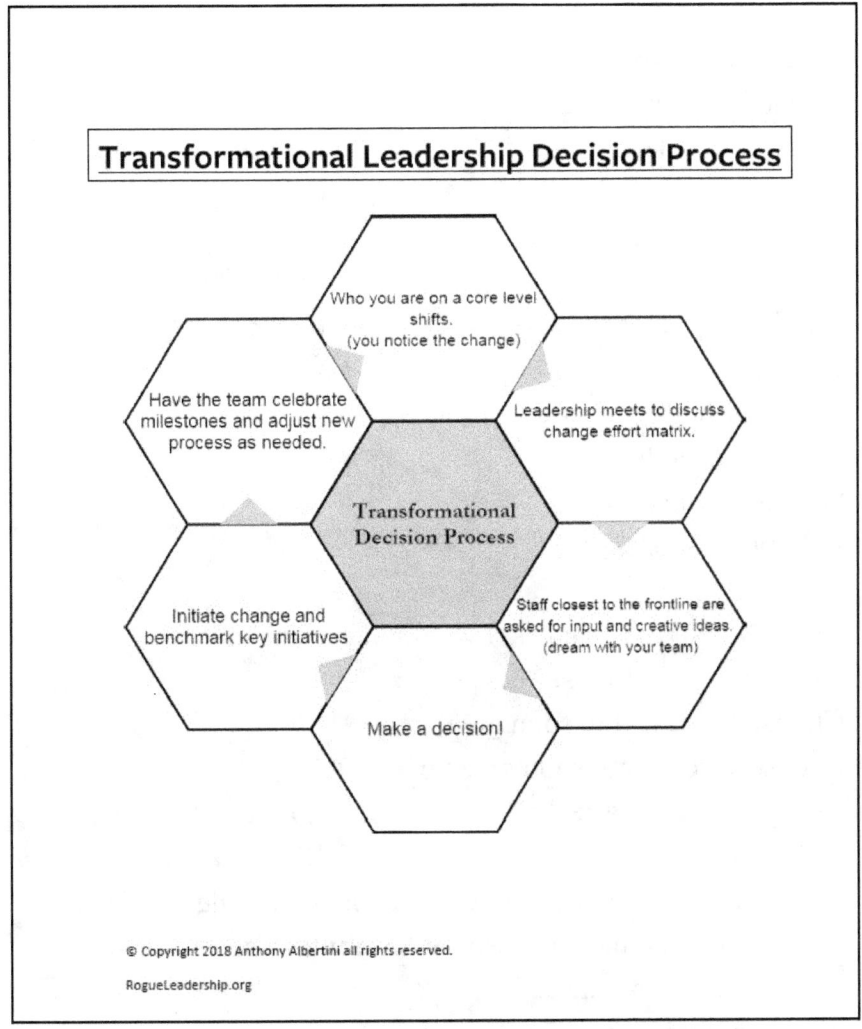

Fig 4

1. Change makes me feel:
   a. Isolated and unfortunate.
   b. Uncertain, but excited.
   c. Frozen and anxious.
   d. Expectant and motivated.

2. When faced with change that is either good or bad on its surface I:
   a. Look for the bright side.
   b. Withdraw and hide.
   c. Seek out, counsel.
   d. Eat my emotions.

3. When I think of the changes, I would like to make I:
   a. Dwell on past failures.
   b. Choose just one, but soon give up.
   c. Choose several, but soon give up.
   d. See the dream as a reality, make a plan and move forward.

4. When I am faced with a major change, the first thing I do is:
   a. Look for others that have dealt with similar issues.
   b. Feel overcome by the task.
   c. Research, research, and more research.
   d. Dwell on all the possibilities of failure.

5. When I reflect on changes in my past, I:
   a. Reflect on the improvements that I have experienced.
   b. Think that others have better experiences than me.

c. Feel accomplished with my life so far.
   d. Feel regret for my mistakes.

6. When I share about a difficult change that I have experienced, I:
   a. identify the root cause of the change.
   b. Explain my plan for moving through any pain I experienced.
   c. List the reasons why it would not help.
   d. Detail my feelings of concern, but show how I moved forward.

7. My friends would say that I:
   a. I am fearless and aggressive in the face of change.
   b. Avoid change at all costs.
   c. Become angry and depressed when faced with change.
   d. Generally, accept change pretty well.

8. During a change process when things get tough I:
   a. Exercise to clear my head.
   b. Sleep/ hide.
   c. Journal, sketch or doodle.
   d. Watch TV, read a book, listen to music, etc. (other escapist activity).

9. When faced with a core shift (real or manufactured change), I look within myself:
   a. Never
   b. Rarely
   c. Sometimes
   d. Often

10. When faced with a change I:
   a. Hold tight to the status quo no matter what.
   b. Grit my teeth and muddle through.
   c. Get angry.
   d. Get excited and hopeful.

Scoring Key - Add up the points for each question to find your change quotient.

1. a. 2, b. 3, c. 1, d. 4

2. a. 4, b. 2, c. 3, d, 1

3. a. 1, b. 3, c. 2, d. 4

4. a. 4, b. 2, c. 3, d. 1

5. a. 4, b. 1, c. 3, d. 2

6. a. 2, b. 4, c. 1, d. 3

7. a. 4, b. 1, c. 2, d. 3

8. a. 3, b. 2, c. 4, d. 1

9. a. 1, b. 2, c. 3, 4. 4

10. a. 1, b. 3, c. 2, d. 4

Total Score _____

How to read your score:

[32 - 40 points] Change Champion
You are the early adopter of change, and you thrive on the process! You keep a wildly positive outlook and are confident that it will be worth it in the end.
Caution- Be sure that your team isn't being left in your dust. It may be hard, but focus on building consensus as you go.

[21 - 31 points] Change Leader
Change doesn't scare you, but you don't have as much time to deal with it as you might need. You accept the need for and your ability to initiate changes. You willingly access people and resources that can help you lead change.
Caution- You can get so caught up in day to day business that you miss the need for change. Stay close to your team and listen to those closest frontlines.

[11 – 20 points] Change Curious

You're not opposed to change, but you don't welcome either. You will tend to drag your toes to see if you can stop change when it starts to hurt too much. You prefer to hide or escape when faced with the challenge of change.
Caution- As a change curious leader you need to surround yourself with resources and people that can help you see the need for change. If you keep your team close and dream with them, the change will surface, and you can keep your anxiety levels under control with their help. You recruited a great team. Listen to them.

[1-10 points] Change Averse
You don't like change! In fact, you despise change in all its various forms. Many people find change difficult and feel a real sense of loss giving up the status quo! You have a tendency to tell yourself, "This will never work!" Your plan is to run and hide from change and ride out the storm.
Caution- Your tendency to dig in your heels and defend the status quo can hurt your organization. Be aware that you will either bury your head in the sand or sabotage change efforts until it is too late.
If you are leading the change-averse, honest and over-communicated need and feedback will help keep anxiety levels lower. This group, when cornered will lash out and try to stop the leader.

"To accomplish great things, we must not only act but also dream; not only plan but also believe."
- Anatole France

    Time to put this whole thing together. I was inspired to write this little book because, after two decades of ministry and business experience, I have seen that our teams are suffering. Leaders need a real and Biblically based system to adapt and change to the world around them. The truth is most organizations lack the skills to adapt. We stick with what we know, even if it stops working. That is called a mumpsimus.

    Does that sound familiar to you? In far too many meetings I have been a part of, it comes out like this: "We must not become worldly, or we have always done business this way!" There are hundreds of variations on this theme, and I am sure you can name many from your own experience. So, the courageous question I want you to ask is this, "What would your organization look like if God were to transform it through you?" In other words… "What color are your Boots?"

About the Author

Andy Albertini is a professional change manager, sought after speaker, and board development specialist. He writes for various magazines, blogs, and at www.rogueleadership.org

Andy frequently runs cohort groups for up and coming executives in the Dallas/Ft. Worth area, and you can find details about attending one (or having one just for your organization) at RogueLeadership.org.

Andy's contact information is located at RogueLeadership.org.

Rogue Leadership

Andy Albertini

www.ingramcontent.com/pod-product-compliance
Lightning Source LLC
Chambersburg PA
CBHW052103110526
44591CB00013B/2325